INVESTIGATING
EROSION

SUPER COOL SCIENCE EXPERIMENTS

CHERRY LAKE PRESS
Ann Arbor, Michigan

SCIENCE INVESTIGATION

by Ariel Kazunas and Charnan Simon

CHERRY LAKE PRESS

Published in the United States of America by
Cherry Lake Publishing Group
Ann Arbor, Michigan
www.cherrylakepublishing.com

Reading Adviser: Beth Walker Gambro, MS, Ed., Reading Consultant, Yorkville, IL

Content Editor: Robert Wolffe, EdD,
Professor of Teacher Education, Bradley University, Peoria, Illinois

Book Designer: Ed Morgan of Bowerbird Books

Grateful acknowledgment to Deborah Simon, Department of Chemistry,
Whitman College

Photo Credits: cover and title page, 6, 7, 8, 12, 15, 16, 19, 20, 23, 24, 26, 27, 29, freepik.com; 4, bvi4092/flickr.com; 5, 9, 10, 13, 14, 17, 18, 21, 22, 25, 28, The Design Lab; 11, Trougnouf (Benoit Brummer)/Wikimedia Commons.

Cherry Lake Press is an imprint of Cherry Lake Publishing Group.

Library of Congress Cataloging-in-Publication Data has been filed and is available at catalog.loc.gov

Printed in the United States of America
Corporate Graphics

A Note to Parents and Teachers: Please review the instructions for these experiments before your children do them. Be sure to help them with any experiments you do not think they can safely conduct on their own.

A Note to Kids: Be sure to ask an adult for help with these experiments when you need it. Always put your safety first!

Note from Publisher: Websites change regularly, and their future contents are outside of our control. Supervise children when conducting any recommended online searches for extended learning opportunities.

CONTENTS

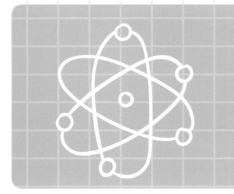

Break It DOWN!

Have you ever visited or seen pictures of the Grand Canyon? It's one of the deepest valleys in the world. In fact, it's so deep that in some places you could fit 19 Statues of Liberty stacked on top of each other! The Grand Canyon was carved out over millions of years by the Colorado River. The process of wearing away Earth's surface by forces such as water, wind, and ice is called **erosion**. In this book, we'll learn how scientists think as we experiment with erosion!

The Grand Canyon

Getting STARTED

Scientists learn by studying something very carefully. For example, geologists are scientists who study erosion. They notice that everything, from rocks to mountains, wears down over time. They understand that Earth's materials get moved from place to place. They do experiments to understand how and why this happens. Scientists write down their **observations** and everything they discover. These observations often lead to new questions and experiments.

When scientists design experiments, they often use the scientific method. What is the scientific method? It's a step-by-step process to answer specific questions. The steps don't always follow the same pattern. However, the scientific method often works like this:

STEP ONE: A scientist gathers the facts and makes observations about one particular thing.

STEP TWO: The scientist comes up with a question that is not answered by observations and facts.

STEP THREE: The scientist creates a **hypothesis**. This is a statement about what the scientist thinks might be the answer to the question.

STEP FOUR: The scientist tests the hypothesis by designing an experiment to see whether the hypothesis is correct. Then the scientist carries out the experiment and writes down what happens.

STEP FIVE: The scientist draws a **conclusion** based on the result of the experiment. The conclusion might be that the hypothesis is correct. Sometimes, though, the hypothesis is not correct. In that case, the scientist might develop a new hypothesis and another experiment.

In the following experiments, we'll see the scientific method in action. We'll gather some facts and observations about erosion. And for each experiment, we'll develop a question and a hypothesis. Next, we'll do an actual experiment to see if our hypothesis is correct. By the end of the experiment, we should know something new about erosion. Young scientists, are you ready? Let's get started!

EXPERIMENT 1

Worn by Weathering

Erosion is the process by which Earth's materials are worn and carried away. An important part of this process is weathering. Weathering wears down rocks and minerals into smaller pieces. There are different types of weathering. **Chemical weathering** changes the atoms and **molecules**. **Mechanical weathering** leaves the atoms and molecules unchanged.

Rust is a sign of chemical weathering. The metal on cars, bridges, or even in rocks breaks down and gets weaker. What makes rust form? Does water play a part in the process? And does the type of water—fresh or saltwater—make a difference? Let's do an experiment to find out! Come up with a hypothesis about water and rust. Here is one possibility: **An object will rust more quickly if it is wet.**

Here's what you'll need:

- 3 shallow dishes that are the same size
- 3 pieces of steel wool
- Rubber cleaning gloves
- A tablespoon
- Water
- Salt
- Tape
- Marker

FACTS!

Have you ever walked on a sidewalk that was cracked or lifted by tree roots? This is called **biological weathering**. At first, small roots grow underneath the sidewalk. Over time, they get bigger and can crack or lift the pavement.

· INSTRUCTIONS ·

1. Use a piece of tape and marker to label the first dish "Water," the second dish "Salt Water," and the third dish "Dry."

2. Place 1 piece of steel wool that is about the size of a golf ball in each dish. Use gloves when handling steel wool.

3. Fill the "Water" and "Salt Water" dishes halfway with water.

4. Sprinkle 1 tablespoon of salt over the steel wool in the "Salt Water" dish. The "Dry" dish should only have the piece of steel wool in it (no water).

5. Let the dishes sit for 7 days. Observe them every day. Record the date and time you do and how the steel wool changes.

6. On Day 7, put on the gloves and take the steel wool out of the dishes.

7. Hold the steel wool that was in the salt water. Try to pull it apart. Carefully rub it between your fingers.

8. Do the same with the freshwater and dry samples.

9. Write down your observations of each sample.

· CONCLUSION ·

Which piece of steel wool looks the most different after 7 days? Does it crumble easily when handled? Do the wet pieces look very different from the dry piece? Was your hypothesis correct?

Water contains oxygen. **Oxidation** is the process by which oxygen combines with other things. When oxygen reacts with iron, something called iron oxide forms. Most people call this rust. Steel is made from iron. This is why we used steel wool for this experiment.

Moisture helps speed up the rusting process. Salt speeds up rusting, too. The rust makes the steel wool weaker. Does this help explain your findings? You've just demonstrated an example of chemical weathering!

FACTS!

In nature, objects don't always have to sit in water to get rusty. Moist air can do the same thing. In fact, some rocks contain iron. When moist air reacts with this iron, rust forms on the rocks.

Freeze and Thaw

Have you ever been riding in a car that hit a pothole? Why do roads get potholes anyway? In places that get cold in winter, the water on roads can freeze, thaw, and freeze again. Could this cause the roads to weather, creating potholes?

Let's come up with a hypothesis to test this theory. Here's one option: **The repeated freezing and thawing of water in the cracks of cement or rocks can break those materials apart.**

There are an estimated 55 million potholes on roadways in the United States!

Here's what you'll need:

- 2 empty 1-pint (0.5 liter) milk cartons, with the tops cut off
- 2–3 cups of white flour
- 1–2 cups of warm water
- Bowl
- Spoon
- A small balloon
- Freezer

· INSTRUCTIONS ·

1. Mix 2 cups of flour with 1 cup of warm water in a bowl to make a paste. Stir with the spoon until there are no lumps. It should be thick but easy to stir. Add more water if it's too thick or more flour if it's too thin.

2. Fill the balloon with water until it's the size of a Ping-Pong ball. Tie a knot in the end to seal it.

3. Pour equal amounts of the paste into each milk carton.

4. Place the filled balloon into 1 carton, and push it down until it's just under the surface of the paste. Hold the balloon down until the paste sets enough to keep it from rising.

5. Let the mixture in both milk cartons harden for about 1 hour.

6. After 1 hour, put both cartons in the freezer overnight. Remember which carton contains the balloon!

7. The next morning, take both milk cartons out of the freezer. What do you notice?

CONCLUSION

The paste mixture represents a rock or road. The balloon represents a mass of water. This experiment recreates what happens when water seeps into a crack and freezes. When water freezes, it expands. Is the paste that contains the balloon cracked? What about the paste in the other container? Does this explain how potholes form? Was your hypothesis correct? This experiment shows mechanical weathering in action.

FACTS!

Weathering isn't always destructive. It can create things, too. If it weren't for weathering, we wouldn't have soil! Soil is a mixture of small rock particles—worn down by weathering—plus **decayed** plants and animals. It also contains lots of small living organisms. Making soil takes a long time. It can take hundreds of years for enough material to break down to create soil that supports a forest.

·EXPERIMENT 3·

Wind Erosion

Weathering has many causes and effects. Do you think the same is true for erosion? Once rocks or other materials have been broken down into smaller pieces, how are they moved around Earth? One way is by wind. So, what factors affect wind erosion?

Here is one possible hypothesis: **Places with strong winds and exposed soil will erode faster than places with strong winds and better-protected soil.**

Here's what you'll need:

- 2 large sheets of white paper (newspaper will work)
- A flat, clean place outside, such as a sidewalk
- Equal amounts of soil, sand, and gravel (or hot chocolate mix, cornmeal, and dried beans) mixed together
- Objects of various shapes and sizes (for example, bricks, cans, blocks, sticks, potted plants, and rocks)
- Balloon
- Ruler

· INSTRUCTIONS ·

1. Lay the 2 sheets of paper on your flat surface.

2. Evenly spread half of your soil mixture on one piece of paper and the other half on the other piece of paper.

3. Set several of the objects on top of the mixture on one sheet. Leave the other sheet as is.

4. Blow into the balloon to inflate it. Pinch the neck of the balloon closed with your fingers.

5. Bend down so the balloon is about 6 inches (15.2 centimeters) from the mixture on the paper with no objects. Use the ruler to measure the distance.

6. Point the neck of the balloon across and slightly down toward the paper. Tightly hold the balloon in one hand, and loosen your grip on the balloon's neck slightly with your other hand to let the air out of the balloon.

7. Inflate the balloon again, and repeat the process with the mixture on the paper that has objects on it. Do some things move? Record your observations.

CONCLUSION

The air from the balloon represents wind blowing across a landscape. How were the results different for each setup? Did the objects prevent some of the material from being blown away? Was your hypothesis correct? Bare soil can erode faster because there is little to keep it in place. Trees and plants have roots that help anchor the soil. Plants may also act as a physical barrier that helps slow the wind.

FACTS!

In the 1930s, a severe drought hit some parts of the United States. This was known as the Dust Bowl. Because of bad farming practices, there were no roots to hold the soil in place or water to weigh it down. This made it easier for winds to sweep the soil away in large dust storms. The drought killed crops and forced millions of people to move.

EXPERIMENT 4

Glaciers in Action

Glaciers are masses of ice that are very thick and large. Thousands of years ago, many parts of the world were covered by these slow-moving rivers of ice.

Some glaciers traveled south from Canada into parts of the United States. Could glaciers have something to do with the movement of soil and rock? Here is one possible hypothesis: **Glaciers can push ahead or carry along materials such as soil and rock and leave them in another location.**

Here's what you'll need:

- A book
- Modeling clay
- Baking sheet
- 2 small bowls
- Ice cubes
- Soil
- Sand

· INSTRUCTIONS ·

1. Flatten the clay into a thin layer across the baking sheet. Leave a strip of bare space at one end of the sheet.

2. Use your book to prop up the end of the baking sheet so the sheet is slightly raised at an angle.

3. Sprinkle some of the soil and sand on top of the clay.

4. Put a bit of leftover sand in 1 bowl.

5. Place an ice cube on top of the sand in the bowl. Leave it there until some of the sand sticks to the cube.

6. Pick up the ice cube and rub it, sandy side down, on the clay at the top of the baking sheet. Observe how this affects the clay underneath it.

7. Release the ice cube and let it slide down the length of the sheet. What happens to the soil and sand? Let the ice cube travel all the way down the sheet, until it stops in the bare space. What do you notice about the ice cube? Record your observations.

8. Place the ice cube in the second bowl, and let it melt completely. Examine the water it leaves behind.

CONCLUSION

What did rubbing the sandy ice cube do to the clay? Did anything move with the ice cube when it flowed down the sheet? Was there anything in the water when the ice cube melted? Think of the ice cube as a mini-glacier. A real glacier can move much larger objects and scrape deep into Earth's surface. Some glaciers have even dug out areas that became lakes. If a glacier melts, deposition may occur. Deposition is when materials from one location are left in another location. Does this help explain your results? Was your hypothesis correct?

FACTS!

Deposition happens everywhere, even in caves! Some of the gases present in water can form substances that dissolve rock. That rock is then carried along with the water until it drips from a cave ceiling and **evaporates**. Over time, this process deposits enough rock to create amazing formations called stalactites or stalagmites.

EXPERIMENT 5

Watch Out! Landslide

If you've ever seen a landslide on TV or in a movie, you might have noticed a lot of soil or rock matter rushing down a slope. Heavy rains can trigger some types of landslides. Do you think the steepness of a slope also affects a landslide? Let's find out.

Here are two hypotheses we can test:

Hypothesis #1: The steeper the slope of a hill, the easier it will be for water to move soil and rocks down that slope.

Hypothesis #2: The steepness of the slope of a hill will have no effect on how easy it is for water to move soil and rocks down that slope.

Here's what you'll need:

- Masking tape
- Paper cup with holes punched in the bottom
- 2 half-gallon (1.9 L) milk cartons
- Scissors
- 2 baking sheets
- 2 cups each of soil, sand, and gravel (or hot chocolate mix, cornmeal, and dried beans) mixed together
- 4 toy blocks
- Drinking glass
- Water

· INSTRUCTIONS ·

1. Use tape to seal closed the pouring spout of the milk cartons.

2. Use the scissors to cut away an entire side panel of 1 carton. Cut out the bottom, too. Do the same with the other carton.

3. Lay one carton on each baking sheet. The section where you cut away the side panel should be facing up.

4. Divide your soil mixture into 2 equal piles. Put 1 pile in each carton. Make sure the mixture doesn't fall out where you cut away the bottom of the carton.

5. Prop up the spout end of 1 carton with 1 block. Prop up the same end of the other carton using 3 stacked blocks.

6. Fill the drinking glass with water.

7. Hold the paper cup over the raised end of the carton that is propped up with 1 block. Pour the water from the drinking glass into the paper cup. Observe the color of the water as it drains from your carton onto the sheet.

8. Test the other carton in the same way. Sprinkle an equal amount of water over the raised end of the steeper carton. Write down your observations.

CONCLUSION

What happened to the mixture when you poured water over the first carton? Did anything move? What color was the water that drained away? Were your results different for the carton that was raised at a steeper slope? Was more of the mixture carried away? What does this tell us about erosion? You might have noticed that the water flowed more quickly down the steeper slope. Water that moves faster has more energy than slow-moving water. It moves more material. Was your hypothesis correct?

EXPERIMENT 6

Do It Yourself!

Do you still have questions about erosion? Can erosion be slowed or stopped? Use the same setup as the last experiment to find out. The "hillsides" in our milk cartons were bare. What if you planted things such as plastic forks (with the tines in the soil mixture) to represent trees or bits of leaves and small pieces of sponge for bushes and shrubs? Would this reduce erosion caused by water? Come up with a hypothesis to test. Then prepare your materials, write down your instructions, and run the experiment to find out!

Think about erosion the next time you visit a beach.

FACTS!

Okay, scientists! You now know many new things about erosion. You even learned how to come up with your own hypothesis and test it!

Glossary

biological weathering (bye-uh-LAHJ-ih-kuhl WETH-ur-ing) the wearing down of rocks and minerals caused by plants and animals

chemical weathering (KEM-uh-kuhl WETH-ur-ing) the wearing down of rocks and minerals due to changes in their chemical makeup

conclusion (kuhn-KLOO-zhuhn) a final decision, thought, or opinion

decayed (dih-KAYD) rotted

erosion (ih-ROE-zhuhn) a gradual eating or wearing away by wind, water, or glaciers

evaporates (ih-VAP-uh-rayts) turns from a liquid into a gas

hypothesis (hy-POTH-uh-sihss) a logical guess about what will happen in an experiment

mechanical weathering (muh-KAN-uh-kuhl WETH-ur-ing) the breakdown of rocks or other materials through physical means, such as water freezing in a crack in a rock, and not through a chemical change

molecules (MOL-uh-kyoolz) tiny building blocks that make up everything

observations (ob-zur-VAY-shuhnz) things that are seen or noticed with one's senses

oxidation (ok-si-DAY-shuhn) a chemical change that involves the transfer of small particles called electrons or oxygen

For More Information

BOOKS

Baby Professor. *Where Do Small Rocks Come From? Erosion and Weathering*. Newark, DE: Speedy Publishing, 2021.

Pattison, Darcy. *Erosion*. Little Rock, AR: Mims Books, 2020.

Vestal, Meghan. *Geology for Kids*. Emeryville, CA: Rockridge Press, 2020.

WEBSITES

Explore these online sources with an adult:

Britannica Kids: Erosion

NASA: Honey, I Shrunk the Beach!

PBS Kids: Nature WY—Erosion

Index

About the Authors

Ariel Kazunas is a writer who has worked for several nonprofit magazines. A graduate of Lewis and Clark College, she lives in Portland, Oregon, where she tends to her vegetable garden—and everything that goes into creating and protecting the soil in which it grows!

Charnan Simon is a former editor of *Cricket Magazine* and the author of more than 100 books for young readers. She lives in Seattle, Washington, and is learning more about chemistry every day.